Funny Incidents

or, why no good deed goes unpunished!

Kay Morrison

~ A Book of True Stories, Too Funny Not to Share! ~

Funny Incidents or, why no good deed goes unpunished!

Copyright © Kay Morrison, 2022

The author has asserted her moral rights

First published in Ireland, in 2022, under the imprint of The Manuscript Publisher

ISBN: 978-1-911442-38-7

A CIP Catalogue record for this book is available from the National Library

Typesetting, page design and layout by DocumentsandManuscripts.com

Cover design by Karolina Smorczewska

Published, printed and bound in Ireland

Funny Incidents or,

why no good deed goes unpunished!

Acknowledgement

I would like to thank my son, Richie Morrison, for all his help with this book.

Foreword

This is dedicated to all my family and friends, who have given me many laughs over the years. Also, to all the people who gave me permission to use their little funny stories here – enjoyed them all. Thank you.

I decided to compile a collection of true, funny stories and incidents to cheer myself up. I wanted to be able to share them with others and, hopefully, make them smile. Through the media and through my friends and family, I have invited people to send me in their funny stories and I did not adjust them. I wanted people to share with us their Irish sense of humour. So read them as they occurred from the original source.

The first few are from me and I am delighted to be able to tell people of the occasions that stick out in my mind. Every time I remember them, I still laugh (and sometimes cringe). Some say that I should have been called Calamity Jane. These are the sort of things that happen to you and you cannot ever forget about them. They sort of follow you around for the rest of your life, like a bad smell, handed down through the generations and anyone else that are willing to listen to you. I hope you enjoy reading them just as much as I had collecting them.

There has been great laughter, here in this house, just discussing all of these stories that I have gathered and I'm sure you'll get a giggle out of them. Some of the best stories could not be told here... maybe for the next book, if I get the nerve and a stiff drink!

I annoyed everyone over the past few years, always asking them for their memories that I could use in this collection. Getting these stories was like pulling teeth sometimes – hard at the time but, definitely worth it in the end. It took me quite a while to finish it but, I'm glad that I did. Thanks for all the laughs!

So here we go...

Contents

Acknowledgement i

Foreword iii

From Kay in Dún Laoghaire 1

The Flight of the Earls 3

The Hubby's Hair Disaster 7

The Collar 9

The Teeth 11

The Stockings 13

The Teacher 14

How Did You Guess? 16

The Birthday Cake 17

The Bank 19

The Grim Reaper 20

**Now Some Stories from You All... ** 21

Mary from Monkstown 23

Mary from Monkstown 24

Rose from Scotland 25

Rose from Scotland 26

Tony from Galway 27

Tony from Galway 28

Deirdre from Dublin 29

Catherine from Loughlinstown 30

Tina from Ballyoden 31

Bookshop owner from Blackrock 32

John from Dún Laoghaire 33

Marian from Dalkey 35

John from Sallynoggin 36

John from Loughlinstown 37

Pat from Santry 38

Pat from Santry 39

Pat from Santry 40

Patricia from Ballybrack 41

Kay from Dún Laoghaire 42

Johnie from Drogheda 44

Catherine from Sandyford 45

Johnie from Drogheda 46

Johnie from Drogheda 47

Tony from Galway 48

Terrance from Widnes, England 49

Susan from Glenageary 50

Tony from Claregalway 51

Darren from Finglas 52

Graham from Italy 53

Another Two from Me.. 55

    The Safety Pin 57

    Hairdressers, Blackrock.............................. 59

A Few More from You 61

    Helen from Monkstown.............................. 63

    Helen from Monkstown.............................. 64

    Anne from Loughlinstown 65

    Anne from Loughlinstown 66

    Patrick from Castleknock 67

    Patrick from Castleknock 68

    Stephen from Drogheda 69

    Darren from Dún Laoghaire 70

    Terry from Ashgrove, Dún Laoghaire..................... 72

A Few Poems that I Have Written over the Years 73

    The F… Word 75

    Second Chance 76

    Postman Pat 77

    My Psychiatrist Said 78

    Recycling.. 79

    Homecoming 80

    I Just Got Me Money Back 81

    Hypochondriac 82

About the Author... 83

From Kay in Dún Laoghaire

The Flight of the Earls

*The first little story that I have to tell you about is so
bizarre that I cannot believe that it actually happened
to me. It is the first incident that I can recall in school
that made me feel embarrassed (I'm sure there were
many more). I have told all my family and friends this
one so read on and enjoy this story.*

I was only twelve at the time and attending Dominican
Convent Primary School in Dún Laoghaire. I loved
writing essays and I loved Art. I got away with
Mathematics okay but I was useless at History. I could not
retain dates of any battle and I had not got a clue about
who fought in any battle at anytime, anywhere. I didn't
care less either. Who needed it anyway? When I knew we
were having a History class, I would develop a bad tummy
ache or I would mitch from school, sometimes with some
of my friends.

On this day, our class were doing important tests to see if
we were suitable to pass on to secondary school.
Everything was going well until it came to the history test.
The teacher put up a few titles to choose from on the
blackboard. If I recall correctly, they were the Flight of
the Earls, the 1916 Rising, the Battle of the Boyne and the
Irish Civil War.

Our teacher announced, "If you want to get points, write
something down on the paper. You will get points for
attempting them so write anything down."

I took her literally, so after looking closely at my options,
I choose the Flight of the Earls. Even though I did not
have a clue about it, it was the best of a bad lot. I did not

have a notion about any of them at all but I thought I would give this one a try and, maybe I would get some points.

I got well into it and in no time at all I handed in my completed paper. I remember I said to my friend, Betty that, "I think it went well" and thought, *Surely, I should get good points for at least attempting it.*

The next day, our teacher gave us all other work to do as she was correcting the test papers at her desk. The quietness was disrupted when we were all shocked to suddenly hear the teacher let out an unmerciful cry. "Would someone get me a glass of water please?" she gasped.

We all knew what this meant – one of us was in serious trouble! The next thing that she did was to go next door to invite the teacher in the adjoining room in to listen to this story. I laughed to my friend but the smile was soon wiped off my face when our teacher returned and I was requested to stand on top of my desk to read out the offending essay: MY ESSAY!? So I did and it went something like this…

"THE FLIGHT OF THE EARLS," I announced loudly.

It was a lovely sunny day, in the middle of spring. There was just a little breeze rustling the green leaves. The centre of Dublin was quiet that day, which was just as well as a large crowd of Earls were on a bus, travelling into Dublin Airport to catch a flight to England. The traffic was light, so it did not take them long. They were never on a flight before and were all really looking forward to it. When they arrived on time, they made their way through the airport with ease. Some of them even had time to go through duty free to buy their bottles of whiskey, cigarettes and perfume for their girlfriends.

Before they knew it, they were all boarding the plane with some of them fighting for a window seat to watch the beautiful views below. As they soared through the clear blue sky, they could see the small streams below and the magnificent Wicklow Mountains. The plane was not full, so they had a nice, quiet flight. The cabin crew handed each of them a small complementary meal and a drink and, before they knew it, they had arrived in England. Each of them said it was a great experience and they would certainly fly again. And this went on to be known as, the Flight of the Earls.

I hadn't even finished reading out my essay when the whole class was laughing their heads off, including both teachers. I did not know why, as I thought I had written a great essay! I remember crying and feeling embarrassed as the teacher said that she was going to send it in to *Our Boys*, which was a magazine in Dublin at the time. I never found out if she ever did.

I went home and told my mother that the teacher made me stand up on the desk to read out my story. However, she only felt sorry for me. It was only when I finally read the real Flight of the Earls story, weeks later, that the penny dropped and I realized that in 1607, there was not even a sniff of planes or aircrafts. Hugh O'Neill and his pals would have been surprised to even see a bus going through Dublin city! However, I still think that my essay was good!

Needless to say, I failed my history test and the teacher went back on her word to give marks for writing anything down. I did get one mark – a big fat X right across the page.

The Hubby's Hair Disaster

The next little story I have to tell you about is going back a few years now (fifty to be exact) when I first lived in Dún Laoghaire. I was only twenty then and we were a newly married couple. We lived with my husband's parents at that time. I always washed my husband's hair and cut it for that matter. This was a well-accepted thing to do back then, as nearly all the young people had long hippy hair styles and were afraid to venture into a barber's shop, in case he cut the whole lot off. My husband was a carpenter who worked in the area.

Anyway, there I was with himself bent over the sink in the little bathroom, waiting for his hair to be massaged into a beautiful lather. I reached back to the shelf and grabbed the nearest shampoo bottle, which happened to be a *Head and Shoulders* shampoo in a white bottle. I began to rub it in with great vigour when, after two minutes, my fingers started to slow down and I could not get through the gunge that was now forming in his hair. My husband asked what the delay was and I told him that I was having a little problem and could not understand what was going on with this shampoo. Well next, with his head still dunked in the sink, he shouted at me, "Where did you get that bottle of shampoo? I hope it's not that white bottle I brought into the workshop to get a bit of free glue!? It's in the *Head and Shoulders* bottle?"

I was panicking now, as the more I tried to rinse his hair with hot water, the more it was setting into his long hair.

"Well, it's your own fault for robbing the glue in the first place and leaving it on the shelf beside the other shampoo bottles!" says I, while trying to contain my laughter.

The stream of curses that came out of him that night, as I struggled to get the glue out, I cannot repeat here. It must have taken me the best part of three hours and my dear mother-in-law knocking on the bathroom door, wondering what was going on! I was up against a real battle that I had never come across before. I ended up having to cut some of his hair off, which didn't go down too well with himself. He told me he would never let me wash his hair again.

When we finally came out of the bathroom, he looked like a badger with the mange. The worst part of this story is that before this incident happened, my husband had a lovely mop of jet-black hair. Within days however, he started to go grey. Oops!

The Collar

For the next story, my husband, John, will never forgive me.

We had been out shopping and returned home after a while. I noticed that when he was driving, he could not turn his neck without the pain resulting from years of workplace injuries.

When we came home, he took to the couch and it was clear to see that he was in extreme pain from his neck. He asked me to fetch his specially made surgical collar from the bedroom. That was the only thing that helped him. John was diagnosed with arthritis a few weeks before and he was fitted for the collar in St Vincent's Hospital. He put it on nearly every day.

Well, he was so bad this day that I thought I would be extra nice to him and give his surgical collar (made of soft cotton and covered in a nylon mesh) a gentle heat in the microwave. Just a few minutes, you understand and besides, it would be a lovely surprise to have it heated up for him for a change! I walked into the sitting room and told him his collar was on the way.

The next thing he says, "Do you smell burning?"

I ran out to the kitchen, with him following on my heels, only to discover smoke bellowing from the microwave. I opened the door in a panic to find a frizzled-up object resembling a well-chewed dog's bone where I had put his collar only three minutes before. I just could not believe it and started laughing, while opening the back door to let the smoke out. He followed me out to the kitchen and, when he had seen the situation, he yelled, "What have you done with my F......G collar?".

When I told him I was only thinking of him, he called me all the eejits under the sun and couldn't believe anyone could be that stupid! We didn't speak for a month, had to throw out the microwave oven and the kitchen reeked of smoke for weeks. He never again replaced that collar with a good one and he always blames me. That's what I got for trying to help him!

The Teeth

The next story that I have for you is my favourite, even though it is a little bit cruel! I was working at a certain private hospital in Cabinteely, Co. Dublin called St. Gabriel's. This was a long, long time ago now. As part of my job, I had to fetch up the lunches and dinners from the main kitchen and deliver them to the patients in their private rooms. People including children came into the hospital to have their tonsils or teeth removed, or some similar smaller operations.

Well, this day in particular, Nurse Maloney spotted me coming out of the lift and asked me what soup I had brought up from the kitchen. When I told her it was a lovely vegetable soup, she said to me, "Kay, there is a young woman up there, in room twenty. She has just had all of her top teeth removed and she is so depressed about it. She is crying all the time and refuses to have a thing to eat. Can you go up to her and ask her would she like a nice bowl of warm soup but, whatever you do, don't mention the teeth! She is depressed enough!"

"Okay," says I, as I walked up the corridor. I kept repeating to myself, "Don't mention the teeth. Don't mention the teeth."

When I got to the patient's door, I slowly opened it and entered. She was sitting propped up and weeping but was able to look at me, to see what I wanted.

It was then I said to her, "I'm sorry to disturb you but Nurse Maloney sent me up to ask you, would you like a nice bowl of warm teeth?"

She thought that I was taking the piss and started crying even louder. Needless to say, I made a quick exit!

The Stockings

It was the first day of August. As it was our wedding anniversary, I was going out for a drink with my husband and wanted to look nice. So I dressed up in a nice summer dress and decided to try out my newly bought stay-up stockings.

Off we went on the bus to Blackrock, feeling delighted with ourselves and ready to celebrate. The trouble only started when I was getting off the bus. I felt that dreaded feeling of the stockings slowly but surely creeping down my legs. I struggled, as much as I could, to try to keep them up by sneaking my hands down and trying to hold on to the tops of them. However, the more I walked the more they came down.

By the time we reached the pub, they were around my ankles. I was beginning to look like Nora Batty from *Last of the Summer Wine*! I had to stand in the door of the pub and take them off. I was mortified as there were loads of people looking on. The other half were not impressed either! Our night was ruined. The hold-up stockings were binned after that!

The Teacher

And then there was the time that I was requested to meet with one of my son's teachers in a school in Cabinteely. My son was well known for acting the maggot, making his friends laugh and doing everything that he should not have been doing in the classroom. I didn't say anything to his dad but went to face the music myself with the teacher.

She brought me down to an empty classroom, took out all of his school copies and went through each and every one of them. She proceeded to point out where my son was going wrong. My cheeks were getting redder by the minute and I was thinking to myself, 'Would she ever stop complaining.'

I reassured her that I took all of her complaints on board.

"He will have to pull up his socks and start concentrating more on his schoolwork if he wants to pass his exams," she hissed.

"Oh yes, as soon as I get home, I will make sure his dad hears of this," I lied.

Anyway, this went on for about an hour and I was wishing I were out of there.

She went on, "He tries to be the class clown and to make everyone laugh but I don't see anything funny in these results."

I promised that I would have a firm word with him and hoped that things would improve in the following weeks. I grabbed my handbag and made it clear that it was time to leave. The atmosphere between us was strained to say the least and it was, indeed, time to go.

The teacher walked over to the door to open it and let me out but, to my horror, the handle came away in her hand! We both stood there looking at it for a moment, wondering what to do when she frightened the life out of me by raising up her two fists and started hammering on the door, shouting out for all she was worth. She did not want to be locked in a room with me, nor I with her and besides all of this, I am claustrophobic!

I joined in with the shouting and the banging on the door and, after what seemed like an eternity, we eventually were heard. A kind man came to our rescue and got us out of there. We were both delighted. I then saw the funny side of it and laughed all the way home. I never again went to a parent/teacher meeting at that school.

How Did You Guess?

A few years ago, my husband and I were in Duty Free at Dublin Airport before we headed to Poland, to visit relations. I picked up a bottle of Baileys to bring with us for a present and headed to the counter to pay for it. I handed in my boarding card as requested and paid for my purchase. The young man behind the cash register then said to me, "I see you are going to Poland."

I was totally taken aback by this and said to him, "Do only people going to Poland come past here?" to which he replied, "No, not at all. They go to all different destinations. Why do you ask?"

I thought about this for a while and then I asked him how he knew I was going to Poland so.

He replied, "It's printed on your boarding pass. Who do you think I am, Mystic Meg?" he mocked as we both burst out laughing.

My husband pulled me out of Duty Free and we left the young man and his mate in stitches.

The Birthday Cake

My sister, Rosaleen, who lives in Scotland, was coming over to Ireland to celebrate her 50th birthday with a party down in a hotel in Dún Laoghaire. She wanted everything to go perfectly, as she was bringing over all of her family from Glasgow for the occasion.

She rang me six months before the big occasion and we went over everything that needed to be done in great detail. We decided on a room in a hotel in Dún Laoghaire and what food to order, etc. She asked me to take on the task of ordering the cake and to make sure that it was a good size to accommodate the large crowd that were invited, including her family from Scotland. I went up to a new bakery up in Loughlinstown to order it and described what I wanted, what style and gave them the details of her name and age to have on it.

My other sisters rang around her friends to invite them, to make sure it would be a great night for her. She rang often to check that all was going well, as she was not here to do it herself. I assured her that everything was going well and not to be worrying.

On the morning of her birthday, I went up to the bakery to collect the cake to bring it to the hotel room. The owner looked at me blankly and said that he did not know anything about a birthday cake. I froze on the spot. He checked the order book and it was certainly ordered. He then looked on all of the shelves to see if it had been put away somewhere but there was not a sign of it. He went in and out of different rooms looking for any sign of the birthday cake but, there was no cake to be seen. He took one look at my shocked face and called in the delivery man from outside.

"Can you bake a cake?" he asked him.

"I will give it a try," he answered.

So the owner told me to call back in an hour and he would try to have it ready. I went home in shock.

An hour later, I returned to the bakery and, to my relief, I collected a beautiful cake, (extremely fresh) and fit for any party. It even had "Happy 50th Birthday, Rosaleen" written on it.

When she saw it that night, she was delighted. Little did she know that it was baked a couple of hours before, as a last chance and by the delivery driver! The owner had to serve the customers in the shop so, he could not bake it himself.

I must tell my sister sometime about all the drama around her birthday cake.

The Bank

I was helping my elderly sister, Anne to shop and she asked me to accompany her into the Ulster Bank in Dún Laoghaire, as she had to change a cheque before she went home. I sat in the seat inside the door, giving her a little privacy to do her business.

Next, my sister called down to me, to come up to the cashier's desk as there was a dispute: she did not have any identification with her and the cashier was not going to change her cheque for her. She did not even have an account there either. In fact, she doesn't have a bank account at all. I tried to explain to my sister that this was the policy in every bank but she didn't understand this, or maybe just didn't want to!

The cashier was losing his patience at this stage and said to her, "How am I supposed to know that you are the person named on this cheque? I have never met you before."

I will NEVER forget her response.

She replied to him, "Look, if I give you my mobile phone number, you go out the back and ring me and if I answer, then you will know it's me."

The entire queue, which had formed behind her, then erupted into fits of laughter. I was every shade of red in the spectrum and thought I would never get out of the bank quick enough!

(P.S. He changed the cheque for her, as I had an account there. She did have a point though!)

The Grim Reaper

*(This is the latest thing to have happened to me and it
is scary stuff!)*

I thought that I looked great in my good black trousers and
best black coat. Maybe I should not have matched it up
with black socks and shoes.

So there I was, walking up Library Road in Dún
Laoghaire when an elderly woman, walking a dog, came
out of a side street. She quickened up her step to get on
front of me. I was amazed at the speed that she was
walking, as I could not walk as fast as her.

She had only gone about twelve feet on front of me when
she suddenly stopped in her tracks. She turned around to
face me and said, "Are you going to a funeral or, are you
following me? You are all dressed in black and look like
the Grim Reaper. Don't you be following me!"

I felt like telling her that she was frightening me! I told
her I had no intention of following her and that I was just
going to the shops, minding my own business. With that
she crossed the road and continued on her journey,
looking back every now and then to check on me. She
went down one road and I went down another, happy to
get away from her.

To my horror, we met up again when we got to the
crossroads on the main street but I quickly got across the
road before she had a chance to insult me again! I left her
staring after me. I thought how I would never get to
change out of my black clothes. I have been called many
a thing before but, the GRIM REAPER!?

Now Some Stories from You All...

Mary from Monkstown

I was at a night out with my husband in Castlebellingham, Co. Louth about 40 years ago. Through the night, for some entertainment, the presenter called out certain items that he wanted people to rush up to the stage with. Then we heard him announce that the first two people up to the stage with two redheads would get a prize. Because my husband and I had red hair we rushed up to the stage and were delighted with ourselves, as we were the first ones. The presenter made a holy show of us, as he was looking for two matchsticks! He gave us a prize anyway but we were really embarrassed and had to put up with everyone laughing at us.

Mary from Monkstown

I was invited out to Dublin to a friend's parent's house. After numerous cups of tea, I asked could I use their bathroom. When I climbed the stairs and went into the bathroom, I could not find the light, so I did not notice the toilet seat down. This beautiful pink, fluffy seat cover was on the toilet. It was too late when I realized I had gone to the toilet without lifting the lid and destroyed the cover!

I panicked, took off the cover and washed it in the sink. I then held it out of the bathroom window to drip but, at that time, her dad came out the back door to have a smoke. He could not figure out what was dripping onto his head and, when he looked up, he saw my arm stretched out of the window, holding onto his dripping-wet loo seat cover.

When I finally came downstairs, I had to own up to what I had done and they forgave me. I have been too embarrassed to ever go back again.

Rose from Scotland

We had had a busy day, with all the family over for dinner in our house in Glasgow. So, around eleven o'clock, we went to bed and quickly fell asleep.

A few hours later, I awoke to the feeling of the end of the bed moving. I was really spooked out over this. I woke my husband up and told him that I thought we were haunted. He told me not to be so stupid and to go back to sleep but, just as he said that, his side of the mattress moved under his feet and with a string of curses, he jumped out of the bed screaming. I quickly followed. We watched as the mattress took on a life of its own and continued moving up and down. We were terrified!

My husband got brave then and pulled up the mattress, only to discover my next-door neighbour's missing cat nearly flattened. We rescued him and returned him home. He was none the worst for his ordeal of a squashed night's sleep but we were in shock, thinking that we had shared our bed with a cat.

Rose from Scotland

I went to pick up my six-year-old Granddaughter, Zara from school. She may be only six but, a real character all together.

I met a teacher and she asked me if I had heard what she had done that day and I thought, "Oh no! What now?"

When I got to her classroom, her teacher was only too pleased to fill me in on the story. Zara had left her classroom to visit the toilets and, in the corridor, she passed the Headmistress having a discussion with two Inspectors visiting the school.

"Most of our students are bilingual," she bragged.

On hearing this Zara stepped back to face the Inspectors. "I can speak Irish, as my nan, Rose, is from Ireland and she thought me," she informed them.

"Oh! How lovely, Zara. Go ahead and speak Irish for the nice Inspectors so."

Next Zara said, in a put-on Irish accent, "Thirty-three... Ah to be sure to be sure."

The Headmistress and Inspectors found it hard to hide their giggles!

Tony from Galway

I got a sad call informing me that a friend's dad had passed away. I made sure to be at the church the next night for the removal.

After the Mass, everyone queued up to pay their respects and I joined them. As I was getting nearer, I could hear people say to him that they were "very sorry for your troubles."

Others were saying, "he was a lovely man" and also, "he had a good life."

As I was getting nearer, I was trying to decide what would be more appropriate to say to him and I was getting slightly nervous. However, when I reached my friend, I put out my hand and said, "CONGRATULATIONS!"

He is still looking at me.

Tony from Galway

I was asked, in 1998, to help a lad and his pregnant girlfriend and to teach him how to decorate his newly acquired flat in Belfast's infamous Divis Flats. He was the godson of a friend of mine. The flat had a panoramic view of Belfast, as it was on the 10th floor.

On the fifth morning of "instruction", I was having the compulsory tradesman's tea break and I thought it was a good time to ask how this man got a flat so easy, when the baby was not even born yet. After all, in Dublin in 1998, you would need five children to be high on a waiting list, before even being considered.

His reply astounded me. He said he just put his foot up to the door and kicked it in! I was instructing a SQUATTER!

Deirdre from Dublin

My brother was always getting his words mixed up. When my sister-in -law went into labour prematurely, he rushed her into the Rotunda Hospital, in the heart of Dublin town and stayed with her for the birth.

We were all worried and, waiting on news for hours, we lit some candles.

It seemed like hours had passed when he finally rang me with news. Excitedly he announced, "Mother and baby are doing well. I have a new baby daughter and everything went well considering. Because the baby was born prematurely, they have decided to put her into an incinerator."

Luckily, I knew what he meant!

Catherine from Loughlinstown

I lived beside a vacant house that was thought to be haunted. There had been a few tragedies taken place there, so strange stories were told about the premises. After it was done up, it was eventually given out to a young, deserving family, who were glad to get it.

This particular night, I awoke to the eerie sound of knocking on my bedroom wall. I was terrified and could not sleep for the rest of the night.

First thing the next morning, I went out to my garden when I spotted the new neighbour attending on her garden. I went over to her and asked her had she heard the knocking on the bedroom wall that went... *Thump! Thump! Thump!* then a small break and it would start all over again... *Thump! Thump! Thump!*

I had the new neighbour as terrified as myself. She called her husband out and asked him if he had heard any *Thump! Thump! Thump!* on the bedroom wall through the night.

He looked puzzled and said that he did not and besides, he would have heard because he was up late, playing DARTS!

So, that was the mystery noise that I had heard!

Tina from Ballyoden

I can remember what happened to me on the day of my first Holy Communion and I will never forget it.

I was all dressed up in my lovely new, white dress and was feeling a little nervous. In the church, I got in the queue behind my schoolmates to walk up the aisle. We were really excited to be receiving Holy Communion for the first time, except ...I didn't.

The fussy teacher was trying to keep us all moving along nicely when, before I knew it, she grabbed me by the arm and placed me in the line for returning to my seat. I was so afraid that I did not speak up to say I had not received communion yet. I felt that I had committed a sin, all thanks to that teacher's mistake.

I didn't say anything to anyone, in case it would ruin my day – not even my mother, in case she stopped me going to our relations and I would get no money.

I thought the next Sunday would never come around so that I would finally walk up the isle to get my first ever Holy Communion.

Bookshop owner from Blackrock

I was out on a social night with a few of my friends in Dún Laoghaire. We were standing in a small group in a well-known pub, chatting away when, all of a sudden, this big, well-built woman stormed through us and, slapping my friend on the back, said to him, "Get out of my way, Fatty."

Well, I know my friend carries a bit of weight but I was not standing by and letting some fat-arsed one insult him. So I shouted after her, "I think I saw your face before."

She stopped in her tracks and said, "Oh! Where?"

I got great satisfaction in answering, "In Hick's butchers shop window in Dún Laoghaire, with an apple in your mouth." (This is a well-known pig in the window for years)

My friend blushed and said, "I would like you all to meet my new boss, Helen!"

I was so embarrassed.

John from Dún Laoghaire

I was just settling back to watch a film that I had been looking forward to when the phone rang. It was my mother, Maisie, sounding distressed.

"There is a cat out the backyard with a can stuck on his head and I can't go to bed and leave him like that. What am I going to do?" she cried.

"I will be down as soon as I can," I assured her.

So we went down: the missus and me.

The poor cat had indeed got his head well and truly, firmly stuck in the can. He obviously was trying to reach the last of the cat food at the bottom of the can when he got his head stuck. (An old lady, a few doors away, had a habit of feeding all the wild cats of the neighbourhood).

The only thing that I could think of was to grab the sweeping brush, push it through the back door and jam the cat's head against the fence, hoping that he could pull himself free from the can. It was useless, however. The cat was not moving. Between him and the mother, I don't know who was worse!

We could not go home and leave the poor cat in this situation for the night, as he surely would have suffocated with the lack of air getting in. He was slumped beside the back fence as it was.

There was only one thing for it; so the wife phoned the ISPCA but got no answer, as it was a weekend. So then she took it upon herself to phone the local Dún Laoghaire Garda station. After hearing the dilemma that we were in, they asked for our address. In less than five minutes, a large Garda van pulled up outside, blocking the whole road. I'm sure the neighbours thought that a murder had occurred!

Three burly Gardaí jumped out and rushed in. One of the Gardaí donned a pair of large, padded gloves while the other two stood safely in the kitchen, looking out of the window with the mother in the middle of them. The brave Garda went out to successfully pull the can from the cat's head. We all held our breath. The cat scampered up the wall and away with him.

The three Gardaí left, saying it was the most unusual request they had had in a while … and the mother went to bed happy.

Marian from Dalkey

I woke up one night to find my husband hallucinating from a temperature that he had developed. He had his two hands on the bedroom wall. He was so bad that he thought the wall was falling in on top of us and he was trying to hold it up. I was hoping to get through the night without having to call a doctor.

I went downstairs to get him a glass of water and I advised him to take two tablets to try to take down his temperature. I told him that the tablets were on the table beside the bed. He swallowed them with the glass of water and, finally, went back to sleep.

When I got up the next morning, I noticed the two tablets still on the table and realised that my husband had taken two small shirt buttons that I had left on the table, to put onto a shirt when I got the time. The most extraordinary thing is that the two buttons made him much better!

John from Sallynoggin

I remember a friend of mine telling me of a funny incident that happened to him and his mate when they were doing a job out in The Liberties, in Dublin. They were asked by the old lady of the house if they would like a cup of tea.

John said, "No thanks" but his mate said he would love a cuppa.

The old lady put the kettle on and got a cup down from the dusty shelf. She decided to give the cup a bit of a wipe out and reached up to the make-shift line over the cooker.

To the astonishment of the two lads, she then proceeded to wipe the cup with her big pink bloomers from the line and, when she was satisfied that it was clean enough, she poured the tea into it and then hung up her bloomers back on the line.

The lad had to drink it then, nearly choking on the laughter as he did.

John from Loughlinstown

Myself and a friend called Robert were sent out to do some maintenance work on a nun's convent in the Coombe area.

When we arrived there, we decided to drive to the rear of the building, which was usually the tradesman's entry. We knocked on the back door for a good while but got no answer. So, we then decided to try the front door.

I knocked and, after a little while, the door creaked open. A little old nun, about three feet tall, held the door slightly ajar, and peeped out at us. We tried to explain to her why we were here but she appeared to be slightly deaf. She took one look at us over the rim of her glasses and said, "Wait there and I will see what I can do for you."

She then closed the door before we could explain further. After a little while, she returned with a few sandwiches in a bag for us. We finally got to tell her that we were not down-and-outs but were there to do a bit of work. She finally let us in.

We kept the sandwiches for our lunch.

Pat from Santry

A few years ago, my late wife, Helen and I went to do our weekly shopping in a large supermarket in Santry town centre. We walked around for a while and then decided to sit down for a nice cup of coffee before we did our shopping, in the adjacent coffee shop.

After a short while, we then went into the supermarket to do the shopping. Both of us noticed that there were a few local undesirables walking around. Anyway, we got all of our groceries into our trolley and headed to the checkout. When it came to paying for them, Helen let out a scream: her bag was open and her purse was gone. She cried bitter tears, as all of her waged, to pay for the groceries and bills, were in it.

The manager was called and, in seeing her upset, he brought us both into his office and ordered more coffee for us, to calm us down. In the meantime security walked around the store to see if they could spot the culprit.

My wife was not feeling too well, so I told the manager it would be best if I brought her home. He gave us some emergency groceries without charge because of all the upset in his store.

We were glad to get home and carried the groceries in. The first thing that we saw, when we entered the kitchen, was Helen's purse on the kitchen table. She had forgotten to bring it.

Pat from Santry

I drove a Ford Anglia car a few years ago and I was working in a school on the southside.

I was driving other men home and we were having a bit of banter. All through this, I could hear a strange noise in the car but I could not understand where it was coming from. Each time that I mentioned it to the others, they said I was imagining it, as they could not hear anything.

We drove along Merrion Strand and across the toll bridge. The noise continued. When I got to Gill Street, I could not stand it any longer and I pulled over. I looked under the car... nothing, then I opened the bonnet and, to my surprise, a cat jumped out and ran off.

I had driven seven miles with the poor cat in distress, stuck under the bonnet in the heat. Just as well that I have good hearing and the cat lived to tell the tale (with maybe ONE life short!).

Pat from Santry

When we were much younger, my friend, Kevin and I were on an outing run by C&C, a mineral drinks company that my late father had connections with. It was in the River Shannon area.

When we got a little hungry, we decided to walk to the nearby shop for some chocolate. When we returned back to the venue, Kevin discovered that he had lost a ten-shilling note, which was a lot of money then. He was very upset, as he needed it to see him through the night. We walked up and down the street looking for it, with no luck. Everyone around us were having a great time, except us.

I thought about it for a while and told my friend that I thought he might have thrown away the tenner with the wrapper from the chocolate bar. He had flung the scrunched-up wrapper into the River Shannon when we had crossed a bridge, so we walked back a mile to that area. We did not hold out much hope in finding the money, as we thought it would be washed out to sea.

When we reached the bridge, we looked down at the running water and there, stuck among the reeds, was the chocolate bar wrapper. We could not believe our luck! I got a large stick to help pull the wrapper out and there was the scrunched up ten-shilling note in the middle of it.

We were not long in retrieving it and him spending it!

Patricia from Ballybrack

When we were teenagers, my sisters and I were discussing what to buy each other for Christmas, as we hadn't a clue. We decided to surprise each other and pick out what we thought might suit.

When we went up to bed, just after midnight on Christmas Eve, I gave my sister, Mary her unusual present of false eyelashes, as she has red hair and very fair eyelashes. I could not wait for her reaction and I knew that she would be delighted.

Just as she was fitting them on at the mirror, fluttering the eyes and admiring her new look, there was an unmerciful scream from the youngest sister, Kathleen, who had just woken up.

"What are yis doing at my presents?" she wanted to know.

We tried to convince her that she was having a nightmare but she continued to shout at us that we had gone through her presents. We told her to go back to sleep but she jumped out of bed and ran over to the press, where she had her presents hidden from us. To our amazement, she took out Mary's present of another pair of false eyelashes and then said that she was sorry, as she thought we had taken her present out.

It turned out that we had both gone into the same chemist in Deansgrange and settled on the lashes: mine black; her's brown.

Mary never had the nerve to wear either of them in the end.

Kay from Dún Laoghaire

When I lived in Dún Laoghaire, my sister, Tisha and I enrolled in a dress-making class. I was expecting my first girl so I had grand ideas to be able to make her little girly dresses. On the first week, the teacher told us to go out and pick up a pattern and material to go with it and all the accessories that we would need.

For some strange reason, I didn't go for little girl dress patterns but decided to make my husband, John, a pair of tweed trousers. I choose a lovely grey-coloured tweed with a fleck in it. It was a heavy tweed at that – the sort to take the skin off your thighs. I really enjoyed making them and it took weeks to complete, as we only went to the dress-making course once a week. The waistband alone was about two inches thick with the heavy tweed!

I was so proud the day that I brought the finished product home and presented it to my husband. The pair of trousers looked expensive and posh (and handmade!). He was delighted. So delighted, in fact, that he wore his brand-new pair of tweed trousers out to the pub with his mates that night.

Halfway through his second pint, he noticed a loose thread hanging from the waistband and he pulled it. Within two minutes, he was left with the whole waistband in his hands as he struggled to hold up the rest of the trousers up. He said that he was lucky he was not charged with indecent exposure!

His friends laughed their heads off as he struggled home, holding up the remainder of the homemade trousers. He gave out and told me he would stick to Dunnes Stores trousers in the future. (There's gratitude for ya!).

Johnie from Drogheda

I just have a short story for you but, I think that it is priceless.

As it was a good day, I cut the grass out the back yard and bagged it into two black sacks. I then left the two bags outside our house, until I was ready to go to the dump with them later.

I had only returned to the back garden a short while when my girlfriend shouted for me to come and see what had happened. It turned out that the men in the white van that drive around each area, taking bags of clothes to bring to foreign countries, had taken a shine to my bags of grass and were off with them before we had a chance to warn them that they only contained our grass cuttings.

If only they had stopped to ask, I would have told them but, it saved me a journey to the dump anyway.

Catherine from Sandyford

This story is a little scary and funny.

My boyfriend's mother and father were coming up from Kerry to Dublin, to visit him. So I made sure that my car was spick and span and ready to drive them around, to show them Killiney, Dún Laoghaire, Dalkey, etc. I had the car valeted and I cleaned the outside.

So, the next day, the four of us headed around all the scenic routes and we all had a great time. All was going well until I was heading to Shankill, Co. Dublin. We were cruising along nicely when I tried to slow down and realised that my brakes were totally gone. My boyfriend and his parents were talking away, not realising the problem that I had and I said nothing.

I was terrified that the traffic lights would turn red, as I would not have been able to stop. I changed gears and put on the hand break gently and, eventually we stopped. I was only too glad to send them into Byrne's pub for a pint while I tried to compose myself.

I phoned my dad and he and my brother came up to rescue me. I got a lift back to get my boyfriend's car, which was not the cleanest and we continued on our trip to Greystones.

So much for me trying to impress them. I nearly killed them instead!

Johnie from Drogheda

I have two more for you.

The first was while I was still living at home, a few years ago now. I went up to the bathroom to get ready to go for a pint with the lads and started to brush my teeth. I was brushing away when I got this vile taste in my mouth. I checked the toothpaste to see what brand it was when I discovered I was brushing my teeth with my mother's HAIR-REMOVER CREAM!

It took me ages to get the taste out of my mouth.

Johnie from Drogheda

The next story goes back to when I was a porter in St. Michael's Hospital in Dún Laoghaire.

The Sister in charge called me up to collect a dead body from the male ward. A nurse accompanied me down to the morgue. First, she joined the man's hands and then she covered the body with a white sheet.

We were just about to leave when the body belched. Then, the hands fell apart and, as they fell to the side of the body, the white sheet was pulled off.

The poor nurse screamed and ran out the door hysterical!

Tony from Galway

I was at Mass in Dún Laoghaire Church a couple of years ago and there was an elderly priest saying the Mass. He went on a bit about Elizabeth from the Bible and how she was told to hold on until she was much older to have a baby.

Some people were getting bored at this long sermon but none as bored as the man who, to everyone's surprise, jumped up and, in no uncertain manor, shouted to the priest, "This Mass is going on for far too long. I will not wait a moment longer. I'm leaving."

So, he got up and walked out.

The next thing to happen was that the late Frank Kelly, who plays Father Jack in *Father Ted*, also got up and walked out. He put his hand on my arm and said, "I am so embarrassed. I cannot stay here now. Everyone will think that was me shouting out" and he walked out of the Mass.

You don't see that happen every day!

Terrance from Widnes, England

The funniest incident that I can remember is about my late dad, Christie.

Years ago, it was nothing to take a chance and go out for a drink and safely drive home on your motorbike with a few jars on you.

Well, this night, my dad came out of the club after drinking a fair few pints and met my sister, Kathy. She was tired from just finishing a shift in the local club in Widnes, so Dad offered her a lift home on the back of his Honda 50.

He took off shakily, with the two of them on it and, as he was a big-build man, there was no chance of the bike doing more than a couple of miles an hour. The next thing he knew was that there was a police car behind them with the siren going. Leaning forward, he shouted back to my sister, "Hold on tight, Kath. I think I can lose them."

(He was pulled in rapidly for drink-driving and neither of them having a helmet).

Susan from Glenageary

Myself and a few relations were going to England on the ferry from Dublin. This jolly-looking, slightly intoxicated woman called Marie got onto the little bus that was to bring us onto the boat.

"Oh no!" she exclaimed, "I have just put my handbag in the luggage shute when I was dropping in my luggage. All I have left is this bag, with a new pair of knickers in it and I even forgot to put them on."

She held up the brown paper bag from Primark, for us all to see and the whole bus was shocked.

Tony from Claregalway

We set off to buy a car and typed the address into the sat nav. It brought us to a house and I could see the car in the driveway. So, I jumped out, in my overalls and tools were quickly taken out. There was no number on the house but the Ford Ka was there and, in my enthusiasm, I just got straight into the task of examining it. The NCT[1] certificate, however, was not as the seller had told me but, I put it down to his mistake.

I was just about to get under the car with the torch when a man came out and asked were we okay. I put out my hand to shake his but he refused to shake hands. I said that we were here, as arranged to buy the car.

He said that it wasn't for sale! His daughter, he said, had no intention of selling it!!!!

OOPS!!!! Wrong house.

So we apologized and slowly retreated. The real car was on the next street.

The strange thing is that the car was to be delivered this evening and the engine overheated today, so we can get our deposit back! Stroke of luck!

---

1 National Car Test – a compulsory vehicle inspection programme in Ireland that tests for road worthiness.

Darren from Finglas

To surprise my girlfriend, I arranged to propose to her live on television, on a reality TV programme.

When we arrived at the hotel, there were television cameras everywhere plus, we had to wear portable microphones clipped onto our clothes. The plan was that I would propose to her after the dinner.

Her parents were brought over from Bulgaria. They hid in a room until it was time to come out and surprise her but, before this time came and, mostly from the nerves, I had to pay a visit to the toilet.

I totally forgot about been wired up and that everyone could hear what was going on in the toilet. So, when I came out, everyone was sniggering and I didn't know why. I then went ahead and proposed live on the telly.

It was only later that the crew told me I could be heard in the loo. (Cringe!).

Graham from Italy

I have been going to college for years and have achieved a Master's degree in computers. As a result, I was offered a part-time job teaching computers to a class of eight, in Dublin. I was delighted and accepted the job, starting the following week.

When the day arrived, I made my way to the college and arrived an hour early. I took out my course work and reviewed it while sitting on a swing chair.

After a while, a woman entered and sat down behind me. She seemed to be annoyed at my swinging on the chair and could not wait to tell me so.

"The class does not start for another half an hour. If you had asked someone outside, they would have told you so. By the way, you are not allowed to swing on the chairs! The teacher will be here shortly," she said snottily.

"I know," I answered, "and I am not that early as I am the teacher and have to prepare for the class," I said, as I made my way to the top table.

That shut her up for the night.

Another Two from Me

The Safety Pin

A few years ago, I worked for a blind lady called Betrice. To distinguish the difference between the back and front of tee-shirts, she would put a safety pin in the back, near the collar. I took some of her washing home each week and, to make sure they were aired, I would place them in the hotpress.

My husband had an appointment for an x-ray in St. Vincent's Hospital, as he was having terrible neck pain. I wished him well as he was taken into the X-Ray Room and I sat outside, reading a book.

After a few minutes, the door opened and the two radiologists ran down the corridor, quickly returning with a doctor. I was getting worried now and wondered what was going on.

The doctor took more x-rays and then, my husband appeared at the door in his hospital gown, with a white face and announced to me that they had found the cause of his sore neck: he must have swallowed a safety pin at some time in the past.

I was astonished at this news and went over to talk to him.

"They asked me if I had any clothes on with a pin in it. I told them, no way."

I looked at the back of his black tee-shirt and there was the biggest safety pin you ever saw.

"Where did you get that tee-shirt from?"

"The hotpress," says he.

I told him that he had one of Betrice's black tee-shirt on and that he had to go to tell the doctor, who was busy booking him in for an urgent op.

Needless to say, we had to run out of the hospital after taking up the doctor's time.

Hairdressers, Blackrock

I was going to a special occasion, so I needed a good haircut.

My daughter worked at Toni and Guy in Blackrock, as a receptionist and told me to come in for the cut, as a treat from her. I usually did not like going to her workplace, as I did not wish to embarrass her. Besides, I knew she would insist on paying for it.

After I finally agreed, I went down at the appointed time. Her boss did my hair and I talked away, on my best behaviour (as you do).

Halfway through, I asked to use the ladies then, I made my way back to the seat, where he was waiting for me. I heard a few giggles but did not know why. He whispered to me to look behind me and yes, you guessed it … there was a stream of toilet paper trailing behind me, tucked neatly into my jeans.

I was mortified and thought I would never get out of there! I never went back again.

A Few More from You

Helen from Monkstown

I worked with a girl who was always bragging about meeting new men, and she was never short of a date.

She was all excited about this new fellow in her life and, after only a few weeks, she was delighted and looking forward to going to Kerry to meet his mother. It was all she talked about.

We all waited, with bated breath, for the next Monday morning to get the gory details from her. Well, when she walked into the office, we quickly realised that it didn't all go according to plan.

She told us that he was a postman and had lied about his mode of transport. He had told her he had a sports car, so she got all dolled up going down to Kerry, in anticipation of all the beautiful places they would cruise by.

When she arrived in Tralee, he met her at the train station on his push bike. Then, when they finally got to his house, she discovered that there were only two bedrooms and she had to sleep with his mother for the whole weekend.

That was the end of Mr. Kerryman.

Helen from Monkstown

Myself, Ann and another friend, Margaret decided to go on a cruise. Any time that the three of us went away, we always had a great time. Ann was always the instigator and, even now in our sixties, we were always up for a laugh.

We boarded the ship at Southampton, England and settled into a lovely cabin. We soon realised that the cabin facing ours had three single men staying in it. As the week went on, we got on well with the men and started to play tricks on them – flirting, I suppose, on both sides.

So, one night, Ann and I left two knickers on the door handle of the men's cabin for a laugh. We did not tell Margaret, as she would not approve and besides, she was getting over heart surgery.

The next night, we headed down to the dining room and Margaret said she would follow us after her shower. One of the three men decided to get us back for all the pranks that we were playing on them and decided to dress up as a ghost, with a sheet over his head.

He knocked on our cabin door and, as Margaret thought that it was one of us, back without a key, she got out of the shower to answer the door. Putting a towel around her, she pulled open the door, and nearly died to find a six-foot GHOST there. She ate the head off the poor man and, after she got over the shock, she reported him to the captain.

We then had to admit to her that it was all our fault and she kept a close eye on everything that we did after that for the rest of the cruise.

Anne from Loughlinstown

A good few years ago, I worked in a pre-school in Loughlinstown, catering for three- to four-year-olds.

A new community Garda, called Tom, came to our area and stopped to introduce himself to me. I asked him if he would be interested in coming into the school, to have a little chat with the children and it would be a nice way for the little ones and their parents to meet him. He agreed and arranged to visit the following week.

Just before he arrived, I told the children that we were going to have a visit from a very important person and that they were to be very good and listen very carefully to what he had to say. I didn't tell them that he was a Garda in case it frightened them.

Tom came into the classroom in full blue uniform, including his large hat and gently told the little ones to always hold onto their mother's hand while out shopping and to eat their dinners all up. The children were trilled and listened intensely.

When it was going home time, one little boy ran over to his mother and announced, "Ma, we had a very special person in to talk to us today."

The mother inquired who it was and the little boy said, "Postman Pat".

Anne from Loughlinstown

I went on to work in a well-known office in Monkstown, which helped people to get a job and to give them advice also.

I was a placement officer and one young lad whom I helped stands out in my mind. I was delighted to help him get a start in a nice little job and thought it would be the last time that I would see him.

A couple of weeks, later I went down to Dún Laoghaire, where I got a shock to see the same young man sitting on the ground begging. I approached him and asked what had gone wrong with the little job I had got him a start in.

While we were chatting away, an elderly lady placed some loose change into his cap on the ground and then she pushed a coin into my hand, saying that she was sorry and that it was the last of her change…

CHARMING! And I thought I looked well!

Patrick from Castleknock

My brother, Eamon was always getting into trouble when he was younger, all innocent stuff but he was a real chancer.

I remember the night that we all headed out to our local disco. Yes, the very one that he was barred from for something trivial. When we got to the main door, we were met by one of the cranky, big, burly bouncers.

"You're barred!" he shouted at my brother, as he let us in.

So, as my brother came prepared, Eamon disappeared around the corner, donned a pair of glasses, and combed his hair over to the side. He then strolled back to the main door but this time with an acquired attitude.

"Ah, you can let him in. I know his face," your man says.

Happy days!

Patrick from Castleknock

The same brother, on another night, was not allowed into the disco (nothing new there!) but not to be outdone, he climbed up onto the roof, in through the skylight and fell down onto the dance floor.

He then went out the front door saying to the bouncer, "You would want to do something about your security in there!"

Priceless!

Stephen from Drogheda

A few years ago, I went to Spain with two of my friends for a week and we had a great time.

I had a separate flight home to Dublin Airport but I agreed to wait in the lounge in the airport for the other two, who would be on the next flight after me.

I sat down over a pint and a lovely girl sat down at the same table. We got talking, and she told me she was an airhostess and also lived in Drogheda. She then suggested that we could, maybe, share a taxi back together to Drogheda town. I was delighted with this, as she was beautiful.

We chatted away for a while and I got to know more about her. The trouble only started when she asked me what occupation I did and, for some reason, I lied and told her I was into computers (I really work on the railways). Maybe I was trying to impress her.

Next, she said to me, "Oh very interesting, and what do you use for your Windows?"

"Windowleen," says I (as I don't even own a computer!).

She got up and walked away.

Darren from Dún Laoghaire

When I started working in Dún Laoghaire Shopping Centre, we had men in huts collecting the car parking fees as the cars left. Later on, however, it was decided that an automated system would be better, where you take a ticket from the machine on entering the car park and paying at the pay stations before you leave.

To avoid confusion surrounding the change, we did a lot of advertising around the centre and invested in new signage.

At the main entrance, I was putting out a large sign in a stand which read, *Don't forget that you need your ticket to exit.*

At that moment, an old lady came over to me and said that she didn't have a ticket. I said that was no problem; I will help her.

I asked her what time she entered the centre.

She replied that she was at the hairdressers for 11am and came in then but done some shopping after that. It was now after 1pm and I told her not to worry; I will only charge her for 2 hours when leaving.

She told me she was leaving right now and had not much money. So I said that I will call security and they will let her out for free on this occasion, as it was a new system.

I asked her which level she parked her car on to which she told me that she doesn't have a car; she walked in through the main doors.

I had to hold my laughter in after explaining the whole process for nearly half an hour. I explained that there is no charge for leaving the centre if you walk in, that the sign I was putting out referred to the car park only.

I nearly died laughing after she walked out.

Terry from Ashgrove, Dún Laoghaire

(I left the best till last, and it's totally true!)

A milkman from Premier Dairies up in Monkstown Farm, Dún Laoghaire called Mr. Magee was going on holidays, so he got a stand-in milkman to do his round for him and also arranged for him to collect his money on the following Friday.

The stand-in milkman did a great job all week, delivering the milk and all was going well until the end of the week, when he had to go out and collect the money around the area.

He knocked to Mrs Murphy's door. When he asked her for the money, she looked at the bill and said, "Oh, by the way, my bill was wrong last week. I did not get my butter or eggs delivered as ordered, so I am not paying this bill."

The stand-in milkman scratched his head and said, "Well, I don't know anything about your butter and eggs on your bill from last week."

The woman was disgusted that he did not believe her and the milkman knew that he was getting nowhere discussing it with her, so he walked away. Unfortunately, as he went out the gate, he innocently shouted back, "Go and ask Magee."

The woman rang up Premier Dairies and got the poor man sacked!

A Few Poems that I Have Written over the Years

The F...Word

Face the Future with confidence.
Find a Friend or two.
Fulfil all your wishes for
Fame and fortune for you.
Flush out all your worries.
Fear not what's in store.
Force out all the negatives.
File the nasties to the floor.
Furnish your world with fun.
Flirt with life and pleasure.
Familiarise yourself with faith. Have
Forgiveness in good measure.

Second Chance

A secluded shady forest
Comforts lovers as they meet.
Separate homes, separate lives,
Hiding their deceit.
The love they share is banned by all.
It's with regret they do recall
The vows they made so long ago
Disintegrated, friends made foe.
Now optimistic, though bemused,
This dilemma so confused.
Beautiful people so in love.
Unfit, yet fit like a glove.
At last, new love so strong;
Is this wrong?
Two hearts melting into one.

Postman Pat

I watch him walking up the street
With his bundle on his back.
I hope he has at least one for me
Just lurking in his sack.
He gets through all weathers
With a smile upon his face.
He always delivers his letters
With a certain kind of grace.
He's over there, now over here
As he zig-zags up the street,
Giving a cherry greeting to
Whoever he might meet.
Bills, begging letters,
They are all of a kind
But it doesn't matter at all to me.
I never seem to mind,
As long as it's a letter
He drops in through my door.
Oh the feeling, oh the rapture!
My heart just seems to soar.
Here he comes...
There he goes.
I watch him hurry past,
Cheekily cutting across
My next-door neighbour's grass!
Oh no! Does that mean
He has none for me today?
So that leaves me with only
One more word to say...
Bast...d!

My Psychiatrist Said

My psychiatrist said I should get out more,
Leave my worries behind,
Just close the door.
Let the family fight about who does the dishes
While I go about fulfilling my wishes.
My psychiatrist said,
I should take up a new sport.
Try running, aerobics, swimming
Or go visit a tennis court.
My psychiatrist says,
I should forget about bills,
Rates, cautions, summons,
And those diseases that kills.
I'm not allowed to fret
About neighbours who keep up with the Jones,
That fence that needs mending,
Or that heavy breather that phones us.
That pain in my back is all in me head.
So, I've to keep taking the tablets,
My psychiatrist said.

Recycling

I didn't know the day would come
When I would never get my dishes done.
Between pots, pans, sticking my hands up cans,
I just want to run.
My worktop once seemed to be clear
And my armchair was beckoning near
But now, I must wash, swishle and swash
Cans, cartons and bottles of beer.
I once had a nice tidy kitchen
And I had no reason for bitchen
But with plastic containers,
Bags of paper, who'd blame us
To throw them all out?

I'm only itching!

Homecoming

You were gone so long,
We missed you.
Your presence, or lack of it,
Was noticed.
Hospital stays are usually short;
Yours went on and on.
We missed you.
Long hours spent travelling –
Buses, trains, automobiles,
Anything to get there. Just to see you.
Had to see you.
Family unit broken.
Words unspoken said…
Why you? What did we do
To have you suffer as you did?
But wait… you're improving.
The morning comes, excitement grows,
Flags, banners stating,
"Welcome home".
Crowds gather in anticipation. We rush
Around, preparing your Homecoming.
Here you come. Cameras flash, music,
Tears flow. Never want to let you go.
It's what you've been longing for –
Your Homecoming.

I Just Got Me Money Back

My husband is a lovely guy
But he is the unluckiest by far.
He can't win anything at the races.
Goes off in his little red car.
He could go to Fairyhouse,
Cheltenham or Leopardstown
But, when he returns, it is always the same.
He looks sad and feeling down.
"I just got me money back,"
He says, looking me in the eye.
"I just got me money back,"
As he begins to cry.
"I should have backed them each way,
Not put on a tenner to win."
But as he looks away,
I'd swear I see him grin!
The Grand National has come and gone
And me hopes began to soar.
Maybe this time, he'll win a little,
Just enough for a new mower.
But no, here he comes with that sad old face.
"I just got me money back.
It wasn't a good race."

Hypochondriac

My ticker's beating dodgy
And my future's looking bleak.
My stomach is gone all podgy
And I need some pills to sleep.
My pains are all arthritic
And my headache's getting bad.
My bowels should be scientific
And I'm suffering from S.A.D.
I suffer from smoker's cough
But I've never had a fag.
My blood pressure's going up
And my boobs are starting to sag.
I have an ingrown toenail
And it's looking a bit queer.

My eyesight's slowly fading.
Oh, did I tell you about my ear?
Well I'm going for my appointment
Because this Virus is going around.
At least I'll get some tablets
Till a cure for me can be found.